PEACHTREE

IGUANODON

and Other Leaf-Eating Dinosaurs

by **Dougal Dixon**

illustrated by **Steve Weston and James Field**

PICTURE WINDOW BOOKS
Minneapolis, Minnesota

Picture Window Books
151 Good Counsel Drive
P.O. Box 669
Mankato, MN 56002-0669
877-845-8392
www.picturewindowbooks.com

Printed in the United States of America.

 All books published by Picture Window Books
are manufactured with paper containing at
least 10 percent post-consumer waste.

Library of Congress Cataloging-in-Publication Data
Dixon, Dougal.
Iguanodon and other leaf-eating dinosaurs / Dougal
Dixon ; illustrated by James Field and Steve Weston.
p. cm. — (Dinosaur find)
Includes bibliographical references and index.
ISBN 978-1-4048-5174-0 (library binding)
1. Dinosaurs–Juvenile literature. 2. Dinosaurs–Food–
Juvenile literature. I. Field, James, 1959- ill. II. Weston,
Steve, ill. III. Title.
QE861.5.D594 2009
567.914–dc22   2008043646

Acknowledgments
This book was produced for Picture Window Books
by Bender Richardson White, U.K.

Illustrations by James Field (cover and pages 4–5,
11, 15, 19, 21) and Steve Weston (pages 7, 9, 13, 17).
Diagrams by Stefan Chabluk.

Photographs: iStockphotos pages 6 (Matt Keal),
8 (Andy Diamond), 10 (Peter Malsbury), 12 (Paul
Tessier), 14 (Jonathan Gibbons), 16 (Dan Bannister),
18, 20 (Gary Bedell)

Consultant: John Stidworthy, Scientific Fellow of
the Zoological Society, London, and former
Lecturer in the Education Department, Natural
History Museum, London.

Types of dinosaurs
In Dinosaur Find books,
a red shape at the top of a
left-hand page shows the
animal was a meat-eater.
A green shape shows it was
a plant-eater.

Just how big—or small—were they?
Dinosaurs were many different
sizes. We have compared their
size to one of the following:

Chicken
2 feet (60 centimeters) tall
Weight 6 pounds (2.7 kilograms)

 Adult person
6 feet (1.8 meters) tall
Weight 170 pounds (76.5 kg)

Elephant
10 feet (3 m) tall
Weight 12,000 pounds
(5,400 kg)

TABLE OF CONTENTS

WHAT'S INSIDE?

Dinosaurs! These dinosaurs survived on a diet of leaves and twigs that grew on bushes and trees that existed between 230 million and 65 million years ago. Find out how they lived and what they have in common with today's animals.

LIFE AS A LEAF-EATER

Dinosaurs lived between 230 million and 65 million years ago. The world did not look the same then. Much of the land and many of the seas were not in the same places as today. Some areas were covered in forests. The leaves of the forests provided food for many different dinosaurs.

Toward the end of the Age of Dinosaurs and at the edge of a forest in what is now North America, dinosaurs ate the plants growing there. *Agujaceratops* tore off tough branches, while *Edmontonia* ate softer leaves.

5

FUTALOGNKOSAURUS

At the end of the Age of Dinosaurs, thick tropical forests grew along riverbanks in South America. There *Futalognkosaurus* lived in herds and ate the leaves from the tall trees that grew close to the water.

River forest feeders today

The modern moose eats plants that grow near rivers and lakes, just like *Futalognkosaurus* once did.

Size Comparison

6

With its long neck, *Futalognkosaurus* could reach the twigs and leaves at the tops of the highest trees.

EOCURSOR

Pronunciation:
EE-o-kur-ser

The smallest leaf-eating dinosaurs fed on the leaves of plants that grew close to the ground. *Eocursor* ate ferns and other low-growing plants. It had to constantly watch for meat-eating predators.

Ground feeders today

The modern hare eats low-growing plants. It also has to beware of meat-eating animals, just as *Eocursor* once had to do.

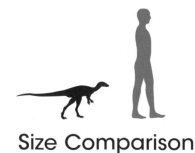

Size Comparison

Eocursor had long legs. It used them to run away from the fierce meat-eating dinosaurs, like *Syntarsus*, that hunted it.

IGUANODON

Pronunciation:
ih-GWAN-o-dahn

Iguanodon lived in swamplands. It moved in herds, eating the leaves of the low-growing swamp plants. Sometimes, *Iguanodon* could stand up on its hind legs to reach the leaves of the trees that grew in the swamp.

Swamp dwellers today

Today, herds of hippos live in swamp areas. They eat the leaves of swamp plants, just as *Iguanodon* did long ago.

Size Comparison

Iguanodon's front paws had a spike for tearing up plants and a flexible digit for grabbing twigs and leaves.

11

HUABEISAURUS

Pronunciation:
HOO-a-bay-SAW-rus

Huabeisaurus was one of the long-necked leaf-eating dinosaurs. It lived in what is now China. *Huabeisaurus* ate constantly, so it had no time to chew food. Instead, it swallowed stones to grind up the food in its stomach.

Stone swallowers today

Some modern plant-eating birds, such as turkeys, swallow small stones. The stones grind up food because the birds can't chew.

Size Comparison

Huabeisaurus had pencil-like teeth that it used to rake leaves from high branches.

PLATEOSAURUS

Pronunciation:
PLAT-ee-o-SAW-rus

There is not much to eat in a desert. Plants grow only at oases, where water comes to the desert surface. Early in dinosaur times, *Plateosaurus* lived near desert oases, eating the leaves of the tough plants that grew there.

Desert feeders today

The modern camel uses its long neck to feed on whatever plants it can find in the desert, just as *Plateosaurus* once did.

Size Comparison

Plateosaurus walked on all fours, but it could also stand up on its hind legs. With a long neck, it could reach the leaves of both ground plants and high trees.

15

GIGANTSPINOSAURUS

Gigantspinosaurus lived in what is now China. It fed on the plants that grew around the lakes. It had a small head, and its teeth were good for chopping up leaves. *Gigantspinosaurus* had plates on its back and big spines on its shoulders.

Spiny defenders today

Modern porcupines use their spiny quills to protect themselves in the same way that *Gigantspinosaurus* once used its spines.

Size Comparison

Gigantspinosaurus' spines would have protected it from big meat-eaters, such as *Yangchuanosaurus.*

AGUJACERATOPS

Pronunciation:
AGU-ha-SER-a-tops

Agujaceratops was one of the horned dinosaurs. Like other horned dinosaurs, it had a beak for pecking twigs and leaves from bushes. Its teeth were good for chopping up the twigs and leaves. Cheek pouches held food while it was being chopped up.

Show-offs today

Today, elk have a big set of antlers. Like *Agujaceratops* once used its shield, elk use their antlers to show how big and strong they are.

Size Comparison

The shield around *Agujaceratops' neck* was used both for protecting the neck and for showing off to other dinosaurs.

19

EDMONTONIA

Pronunciation:
ED-mawn-TOE-nee-uh

The armored dinosaur *Edmontonia* lived at the very end of the Age of Dinosaurs. It ate the leaves of medium-sized bushes that grew in forests. It was one of the last dinosaurs that lived in what is now North America.

Tough-skinned leaf-eaters today

The modern rhinoceros has thick skin and a sharp horn to protect it, like *Edmontonia* did long ago.

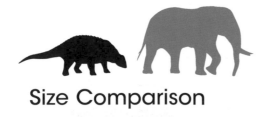

Size Comparison

Edmontonia's armor protected it from big meat-eating dinosaurs such as *Tyrannosaurus*.

WHERE DID THEY GO?

Dinosaurs are extinct, which means that none of them are alive today. Scientists study rocks and fossils to find clues about what happened to dinosaurs.

People have different explanations about what happened. Some people think a huge asteroid that hit Earth caused all sorts of climate changes, which caused the dinosaurs to die. Others think volcanic eruptions caused the climate change and that killed the dinosaurs. No one knows for sure what happened to all of the dinosaurs.

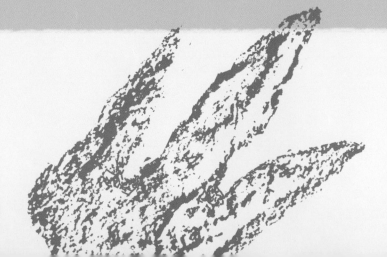

GLOSSARY

armor—protective covering of plates, horns, spikes, or clubs used for fighting

beak—the hard front part of the mouth of birds and some dinosaurs; also called a bill

herd—a large group of animals that move, feed, and sleep together

oases—places in the desert where there is water, often in pools

predators—animals that hunt and eat other animals

shield—a piece of armor

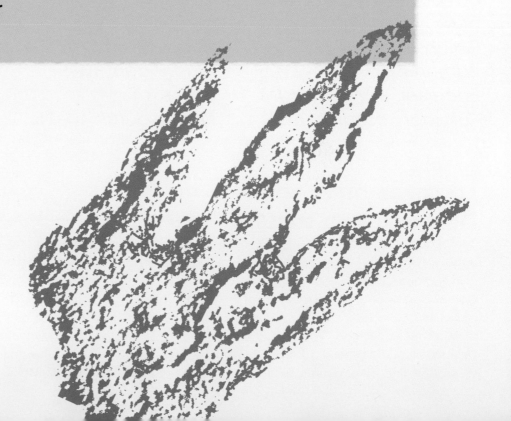

To Learn More

More Books to Read

Clark, Neil, and William Lindsay. *1001 Facts About Dinosaurs.* New York: Dorling Kindersley, 2002.

Dixon, Dougal. *Dougal Dixon's Amazing Dinosaurs.* Honesdale, Penn.: Boyds Mills Press, 2007.

Holtz, Thomas R., and Michael Brett-Surman. *Jurassic Park Institute Dinosaur Field Guide.* New York: Random House, 2001.

On the Web

FactHound offers a safe, fun way to find educator-approved Internet sites related to this book.

Here's what you do:
1. Visit *www.facthound.com*
2. Choose your grade level.
3. Begin your search.

This book's ID number is 9781404851740

Index

Look for other books in the Dinosaur Find series:

Bambiraptor and Other Feathered Dinosaurs

Baryonyx and Other Dinosaurs of the Isle of Wight Digs in England

Camarasaurus and Other Dinosaurs of the Garden Park Digs in Colorado

Chungkingosaurus and Other Plated Dinosaurs

Deinocheirus and Other Big, Fierce Dinosaurs

Diceratops and Other Horned Dinosaurs

Mahakala and Other Insect-Eating Dinosaurs

Masiakasaurus and Other Fish-Eating Dinosaurs

Pawpawsaurus and Other Armored Dinosaurs

Saurophaganax and Other Meat-Eating Dinosaurs

Torosaurus and Other Dinosaurs of the Badlands Digs in Montana

Xiaosaurus and Other Dinosaurs of the Dashanpu Digs in China